THE
Archive Photographs
SERIES

BARNSLEY
IN THE '50S AND '60S

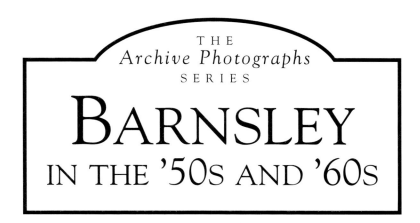

THE
Archive Photographs
SERIES

BARNSLEY
IN THE '50S AND '60S

Compiled by
Louise Whitworth, Gillian Nixon
and Stan Bulmer

CHALFORD

The Chalford Publishing Company
St Mary's Mill, Chalford,
Stroud, Gloucestershire, GL6 8NX

ISBN 0 7524 0644 2

Typesetting and origination by
The Chalford Publishing Company
Printed in Great Britain by
Redwood Books, Trowbridge

Contents

Acknowledgements

Miss Louise Whitworth and Mrs Gillian Nixon would like to thank
Mrs Wendy Hawkins, Miss Nicola Mason, Mr Stanley Bulmer,
Mr Ian Porter (Wilson and Longbottom), Annie Storey, Mr Roy Portman,
the late Mr Sid Jordan, Mrs Pauline Clarke, Mrs Jean Tooth, Mr Edwin Taylor,
the British Waterways Board, the late Miss Nicolson, Vicki Kemp ,
Colin Massingham and Val and Herbert Youel.

Introduction

The era of the Fifties and Sixties is known throughout the world as a period of change and revolution. It was a dynamic time in the history of the world, with notable events such as the Suez Crisis, the Cold War, the Vietnam War and the assassination of President Kennedy high on the political agenda, as well as fantastic events such as Neil Armstrong's walk on the moon and revolutionary fashion statements such as Mary Quant's mini skirt hitting the headlines. Youngsters today are given the impression of the Fifties and Sixties as a time of free love and rock 'n' roll. In England, the early 1950s saw Princess Elizabeth crowned as Queen Elizabeth II, uniting the country in the regal event of the decade, while later on The Beatles were creating a different storm with their revolutionary style of music which would change and influence musical tastes throughout the world.

But how did all these events and changes in philosophy affect the every day lives of the people living in ordinary British towns? Yes, it was possible to go out dancing every night, including Sunday nights, if you wanted to. But did we see demonstrations and revolutionary activities in the community of Barnsley?

In fact, Barnsley was having quite a revolution itself. The Fifties and Sixties was the final age of the 'Old Barnsley' before the face of it was changed for good. Barnsley Market, the largest market in Yorkshire, still took place on Market Hill, where, among other things, cooked meats could be purchased. The Fish Market opposite the May Day Green Market was still in existence. You could buy anything on Barnsley Market and people came from all around the region to shop there. It was demolished in the early 1970s to make way for the shopping centre as we know it today. The Co-op really dominated the town centre at that time; Co-op departments could be seen everywhere and everyone had a 'divi' number to save for either Christmas or holidays. There was also the Arcadian Hall where children were taken to see Father Christmas and have a special meal with waitress service and Butterfield's department store, a fascinating shop, all on different levels with staircases and rooms to be found hidden in every available space. All these places were in their heyday in the Fifties and Sixties and are now no longer in existence.

As for the youth of Barnsley, the YMCA was the place to be. There was a library there and sports facilities and events were organised in a way that made the youngsters feel they were not in the way of the adult population! Most importantly, it was the major meeting place for youngsters to listen to music. And as far as music was concerned, you were either a follower of The Beatles or The Monkees: you had to be one or the other. It was the advent of the pop star and the film *Hard Day's Night* was a sell out at all the picture houses in and around Barnsley. For the first time the youth started to have their own fashions. The 'Beatle' suit was the trend for the boys and 'Twist' dresses for the girls. Flower Power also hit Barnsley and colours were said to explode. Young people were defiantly more fashion conscious and some say they were even outrageous. Hot pants were the big trend in the town at the end of the 1960s and it was the ultimate fashion statement to be seen with a Carnaby Street carrier bag!

On the quieter side of life it had been said that life in Barnsley at this period was more family orientated than it is today and out of town there was still much of the village atmosphere with milk, papers, bread – sometimes the whole weekly shop – delivered to your doorstep by the local grocery store. Local clubs would organise trips to the coast for local families, sometimes by train, sometimes with up to ten or fifteen buses! Not as many people could afford to go on holiday so they took advantage of the club trips and paid weekly throughout the year.

Work life was considerably more industrial than today with the coal mining and iron foundries prominent in the area. But although the employment was secure, the pay was very low. This led to the beginnings of the union action and demonstrations in the late 1960s which were to dominate the lives of Barnsley people in the 1970s and 1980s.

It is easy therefore to see that Barnsley was involved in great change throughout this provocative period in history. Not only did the landscape dramatically change, but the people's ideals and tastes also changed along with those of the rest of the world. Obviously there was no sense of revolution, but the youth of the town started to feel more adventurous and people in the work place wanted better lives for themselves and their families. As with the rest of the world, they wanted to break away from tradition. So, was Barnsley affected by the new world in the Fifties and Sixties? Well, the world went haywire, and it was just too great a storm for it not to be!

All the photographs in this book can be found either at the Barnsley Archive Service or at Stan Plus Stan II, Barnsley. Anyone wishing to look at any of these photographs more closely is very welcome to do so by contacting Barnsley Archive Service, Central Library, Shambles Street, Barnsley, S70 2JF. Tel. 01266 773950

Miss Louise Whitworth
Archivist

8

One
A Time of Change in Central Barnsley

View of Eldon Street taken from a window in the Gaumont Cinema. In the distance can be seen the old Star Paper Mill and the landscape of Athersley and Monk Bretton.

Barnsley Town Hall splendidly decorated for the coronation of Queen Elizabeth II, 1953.

Sunday morning on Market Hill, 1963.

Shopping on Market Hill, c. 1960-1968. Notice the range of motor cars, as seen from the left, a 1960s Jaguar Mk 7, a 1950s Austin Devon, a 1946 Ford Prefect and a 1950s Standard 8.

Queen Street, Barnsley, in 1969. The Three Cranes closed in 1963, with Woolworths gradually taking over the space. In 1972 and 1973 Woolworths built a new store on the same site.

Obelisk House seen here just before its demolition in 1962.

Old Mill Lane Top seen from Church Street, showing the road improvements in July 1963.

View of Gas Nook, between 1950-1962, showing Harry Howe's tripe shop, the Market Fisheries and Metcalf and Manners' leather goods shop. Gas Nook was demolished in 1969 as part of the Barnsley Market redevelopment.

The Wire Trellis Hotel and Gas Nook, between 1950-1962. Originally in the nineteenth century a row of cottages stretched from The Wire Trellis Hotel into Gas Nook and was called Amen Nook.

Barnsley Court House Railway Station frontage, on Regent Street, 1967.

Court House Railway Station in action, showing the north west view, 1956.

The derelict site of Court House Station, seen here in 1967. The station was closed in 1960 as urgent repair work, estimated at £200,000, was needed on the viaduct which spanned Eldon Street. It was decided, at half the cost, to build a new junction to allow trains to run into Exchange Station in the future.

The Gaumont Cinema, Eldon Street, which was opened in 1956. The front doors of the cinema were from the old Empire, which was gutted by fire on the site in 1954.

Interior view of the Gaumont Cinema before it was opened for the public in 1956.

Church Street, as seen on 11 January 1950.

Again a view of Church Street, this time looking in the opposite direction, 1959. Notice the National Provincial Bank, a building which started as the London and Yorkshire Bank in 1875 and is now the Royal Bank of Scotland.

The Co-op has always been a great tradition in Barnsley. Here is the Summer Lane branch of the Co-op in 1963.

The Barnsley British Co-operative Society outfitting department on Cheapside, in the winter of 1955/1956.

This view shows exactly the impact that the Co-op had on the town of Barnsley, with stores and advertisements all around. Throughout its life Market Street has been the home of the Co-operative Society chemist, wallpaper, kitchenware, furnishing, outfitting and tailoring departments, to name but a few. This photograph shows the street as it was in 1961.

Barnsley County Borough Depot, Queens Road. Here can be seen the paint store, offices and miscellaneous store in December 1967.

Numbers 5-9, Park Row, off New Street, seen here in 1961. Park Row was demolished in the mid 1960s.

An imposing view of the Town Hall in 1957, taken from Regent Street.

The back yard of Nos 4-12, Rebecca Street, as seen in November 1963. Notice that tin baths are still prominent, even in the 1960s.

Buckley Street in 1967 after the clearance order. Quite dramatically the Lodge Memorial Methodist church was left standing, later to become known as Buckley Methodist church.

View showing the rear of Nos 64-78, Heelis Street, in 1963. In the foreground can be seen 'the rock', which could not be moved during the housing clearance due to its sheer size and still remains in the same place today.

Wash day in Grace Terrace and Albion Street, November 1963.

Dramatic view of Holy Rood church, September 1968.

Ebenezer chapel with Doncaster Road to the left and Sheffield Road to the right. The Ebenezer chapel was opened in 1873 and to celebrate the event there was a great tea party in the school room. So popular was the opening that the room was packed with people 'from floor to ceiling'. (*Barnsley Chronicle* 11 October 1873).

A view of a derelict Sheffield Road seen here, *c.* 1969. Cantors furniture store had been in operation from 1953 and the Barnsley British Co-operative Society Funeral Service since 1940.

Men at work: two views showing the re-surfacing of Sheffield Road, outside the Ebenezer chapel in May 1954.

In this photograph can be seen The Manx Arms, the public house of many names. In previous years it had been known as the Baltic Inn, the Cricketers Arms and the Legs of Man!

Sheffield Road, showing Nos. 179 and beyond, taken from Park Road traffic lights, November 1963.

Sheffield Road again, this time showing the Spotted Leopard Inn, a licensed premises from 1868.

Numbers 2-6, Court 1 off Park Road, November 1963, an area which has since been redeveloped.

Chances are that views like these will never be seen again in Barnsley. In 1963 this was the junction of Heelis Street and Winn Street.

Another view in 1963. This was Park Terrace, as seen from Grace Street, showing how little space families had to call their own.

Who can remember this Tennants beer store at the end of Wood Street and on the corner of Harry Terrace?

Bateman's Yard, showing rear views of Red House and Redena House, in November 1960. Red House was where John Wilson, the linen manufacturer used to live and Wilson's linen warehouse was formerly in this yard, in 1777.

The former rectory on Church Street, as seen in 1957.

Shambles Street in the 1960s. The Pinfold Steps can be seen just off centre. Who remembers having a pint of Wilson's Bitter?

The Odeon at the Alhambra, in its last week in the 1960s. Stan Bulmer, the projectionist, was showing *The Entertainer* with Laurence Olivier (the title Sir came later).

A view of the Pavilion Cinema after the fire which destroyed it in 1950. Previously, this building housed the Olympia Skating Rink, and became the Pavilion Cinema in 1920.

A look at some classic cars on Dodworth Road, July 1968.

Dodworth Road again, looking towards Broadway junction, in December 1953. This area looks completely different now with overhead traffic lights at the junction and a petrol station on the right hand side. The lady in the centre of the photograph would have a much harder task crossing the road today.

A variety of 1950s vehicles at the bottom of Regent Street, February 1950. To the right can be seen the Queens Hotel, a magnificent building, first opened in 1872 and to the left the Court House Station can just be seen, with the railway bridge going over the road.

More transport of the 1950s. This time a Leyland bus, No. 845, is seen on Kendray Street in 1959.

Pontefract Road and town centre demolition in December 1969.

The building of the new Tesco premises on Albert Street East, January 1967. This building is now part of the modern Boots on Cheapside.

Two scenes of Barnsley over the roof tops. This first photograph shows a grand view of the Town Hall, the Co-op chimney and to the right, Regent Street Congregational church. In the foreground can be seen Heelis Street with a lone see-saw in the playground in 1967.

This second view is actually from the Town Hall tower, looking north east towards the outskirts of Barnsley in 1969.

Two
Playground Antics

A young and obviously very excited Stanley Bulmer (second from the left), seen here outside Worsbrough Common Junior and Infants School.

A former class room, used in the old rectory on Church Street, seen here in 1957.

The staff of Edward Sheerien School, 1960.

A few cheesy grins here from the class of 1959-1960, St Matthew's School, Barnsley. Seen here from left to right are S. Taylor, M. Richards, C. Lumb, D. Brently, H. Allsopps, D. Thompson, M. Hislop, S. Jones, D. Williams, S. Wood, J. Whitehead, S. Green, K. Gibson, R. Bolton, M. Charlesworth, G. Oxtaby, P. Mattrick, E. Wadsworth, E. Fieldsend, A. Mitchell, S. Paul, E. Sherill, C. Hellewell, S. Lawson, P. Hirst, L. Gosling, L. Suddaby, S. Bastow, K. Dorman, S. Wainwright, P. Young, J. Pinner, P. Watts, D. Bamford and D. White.

A view of Blackburne Lane Infants School, which was later to be replaced by St Matthew's Infants. This building is now the Polish Club.

St Matthew's Infants School on Pogmoor Road, sometime in the 1960s.

Apparatus and exercise lessons at St Matthew's School. The young boy in the middle of this photograph looks a bit precariously balanced!

These girls demonstrate their elegance as they pose for this photograph.

This cheeky crowd obviously love going to school and are very pleased to be having their photograph taken.

This looks like fun! R. Smith, E. Blackburne and R. Billingham enjoy playing with water in 1958.

A leaning tower of Pisa? Two boys show off their collection of match boxes here, in 1961.

Who needs to read newspapers when they can be put to much better use? These two girls show off their paper hats in July 1958.

Two photographs here of the May Day and Queen's Coronation celebrations, at Shroggs Head School, Darfield, 1953.

The May Queen has just been crowned and the children sing a song to celebrate. Judith Hopkinson stands slightly out of line, while Russell Boyes grins happily on the left hand side of the row.

Class of 1951, Shroggs Head School, Darfield.

Sports day at St Matthew's, 1957. Just look at the concentration on their faces! Who won the race that day?

Here we see the lovely Mary and Joseph, alias Louise Suddaby and Stephen Green, ready and waiting to star in their 1959 Christmas Nativity Play.

A group of *Just William* lookalikes. What japes did these lads get up to on this Naturalist and Scientific Society ramble to Gunthwaite on 24 June 1950?

Three

Felons, Fire and Flashing Lights

Extinguishing a fire at Dodds in Stairfoot.

The ambulance garage frontage in 1962. This shared the same site as the fire station at Broadway.

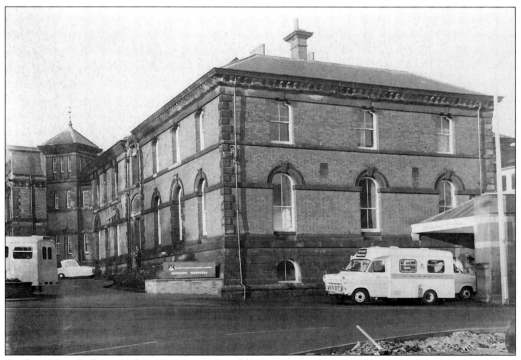

Beckett Hospital opened in 1865 and closed 112 years later in 1977.

Wesley Street, Barnsley; the side of the Alhambra Theatre can be seen on the left.

Parade of the York and Lancaster Regiment when they were given the Freedom of the Borough in 1963.

Damping down a fire at the glass works at Stairfoot in the Sixties.

Firemen pose for the camera after clearing up at the glass works fire at Stairfoot.

Smiling their best smiles are the duty watch at Broadway Fire Station. Mr Oxley was then in charge as station officer.

Now they're showing off their fire engines (and of course the turn-table ladder on the left).

Come on lads, show the cameraman how it's done!

The leading fireman makes sure that the hoses are put back in regulation order.

Some of Barnsley's policemen line up outside the Barnsley British Co-operative Society nursery department in Wellington Street.

Four of the Barnsley Borough's firemen dealing with an accident late at night.

Checking that the harness rope moves smoothly through the pulley on the turntable ladder. The checks are being made at Broadway Fire Station.

Returning the equipment to operational standard after an incident.

This photograph shows the activities of Civil Defence Week, in the Town Hall car park, in around 1957. From the left are Bernard Gorse and Dave Storrs. These men were part of the AFS (Auxiliary Fire Service).

Part of the Auxiliary Fire Service on a map reading exercise, between 1959-1960. Left to right are: a colleague from the Sheffield AFS, Wendy Wildsmith, Val Maxfield, Jean Neesam and Julie Beard.

The floats assembling for the Mayor's Parade in 1969.

Cleaning up after a hayfield caught fire.

A school visit to the fire station at Churchfields in Barnsley. Is this the Dennis Big Six pump escape of the 1930s?

This young girl is still wary of the hose pipe, even with the help of the officer.

This young chap is getting in some practise for when he's old enough to join!

Four
The Rock 'n' Roll Years

Barnsley's 'Mr Music', Geoff Haigh and his orchestra, seen here playing at the Arcadian Hall. Geoff also played at other venues such as The Three Cranes and The Barnsley Baths. Geoff celebrates sixty years of music-making in 1996.

Nations of the Commonwealth, Shafton Coronation Gala.

Shafton Coronation Gala Queen and attendants.

Here we can see two examples of 1950s and 1960s weddings in Barnsley. This photograph is of Sheila Austin's wedding in the late 1950s.

A wedding in the 1960s and notice the change in fashion styles. The short skirts of the 1950s have given way to long caftan-type gowns in the 1960s. A wonderful day for all concerned.

Happy families here at a 1960s christening. Note the building of the police station in the background. This photograph was taken from the rear of Churchfields.

Stanley Bulmer Junior handing over toys for the Odeon Christmas Appeal. The mayor is Alderman Fred Elliott JP, and the time is Christmas 1961.

Easter Bonnet Parade at the Barnsley National Reserve Club in the 1950s.

This plane came down in Worsborough High School grounds in the 1960s. The RAC had to come out to the rescue!

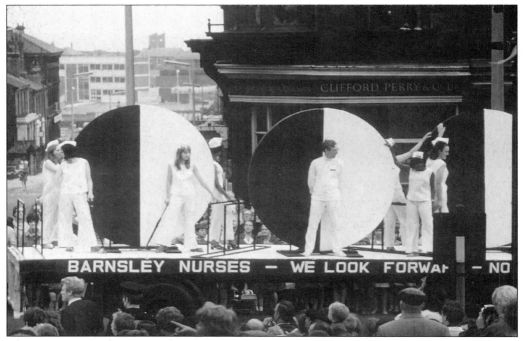

The Mayor's Parade, 1969. This year was the Borough's year of centenary celebrations. The mayor for 1969/1970 was Alderman T. Hinchcliffe JP.

The Mayor's Parade in 1969.

The BXL float in the 1969 Mayor's Parade.

Again the Mayor's Parade in 1969. This time we see the fire brigade participating in this popular annual event.

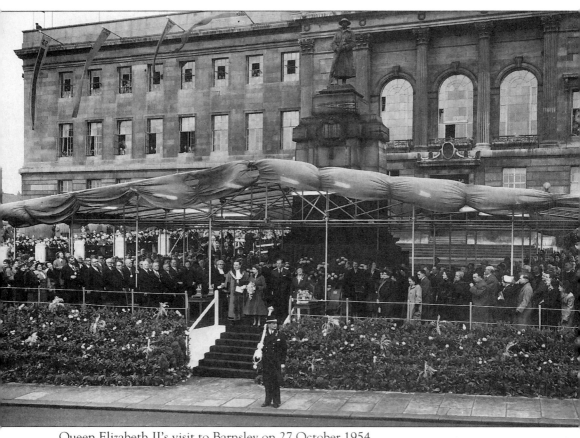

Queen Elizabeth II's visit to Barnsley on 27 October 1954.

Presentation to Queen Elizabeth II, 27 October 1954. Prince Philip is on her left and the Mayor Alderman, Alfred Edward McVie CBE, JP is also on her left. To the right is A.E. Gillfillan, Town Clerk, with the mayoral mace.

Queen Elizabeth II on a drive through Barnsley in 1954. This photograph was possibly taken on Kendray Hill.

The Mayoral Inauguration Parade of Alderman Harry Dancer in 1962 on its way to the civic service on a Sunday morning.

Parading on Remembrance Sunday, 1962 or 1963. The advertisements all around give an indication of the date. You can see that it still only cost forty-four shillings to go to London by train.

Remembrance Sunday Parade. Members of the Territorials and The British Legion are following behind.

Fire and police personnel parading on Remembrance Sunday, 1962 or 1963. Bill Hodges, Ken Farmer, Colin Clegg, Ben Gregory, Eddie Knowles, George Cooper, Mac McDonald and Eddie Broadhead are the names known.

Pogmoor Feast in July 1953 or 1954. These are The Two Waldix, the tightrope walkers.

Part of the tradition of the Pogmoor Feast was Tommy Treddlehoyle. In the parade to Town End and back, Tommy would sit facing backwards on a donkey. Does anyone know how this originated?

Sadly the ground on which Pogmoor Feast was held was sold. A housing estate now occupies this site.

Barnsley FC, in the mid 1960s, at the Queens Road training ground. Jock Steel was the manager, seen at the far right, and other known names are Billy Houghton, Wood and Hough.

Barnsley FC again, this time in a shot taken at Bawtry, Christmas 1951.

Young hopefuls of the Worsbrough Common School football team. Kneeling down in the middle, with the smiling face, is Stan Bulmer Junior.

Nativity Play 1959, possibly performed by the Cudworth Girls Guild at St George's Hall.

Barnsley St Mary's church choir singing for the patients at Beckett Hospital, Christmas 1953.

East or west? These Barnsley folk headed west to Blackpool for their hard earned rest.

Soaking up the sun in their deckchairs at Blackpool are these good people of Barnsley.

Pogmoor Feast, 1953. Here we can see the parade of floats passing Townend Park. Note part of the Canister Company works in background.

Church parade for Barnsley Borough's Centenary, 1969.

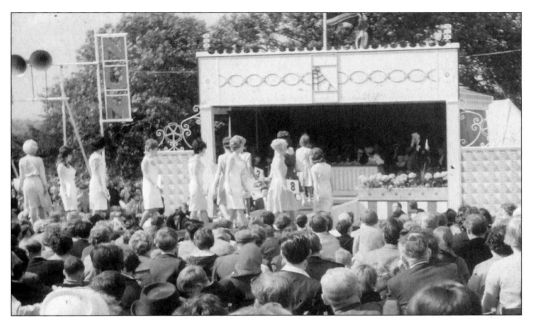

Miners' demonstration and Coal Queen contest, June 1965, presumably held in Locke Park. We wonder who the winner was?

Miners' demonstration and Gala, Locke Park, June 1965.

Johnnie Johnson's Quintet in the 1960s, in Johnnie's home. They were the regular attraction at The Three Cranes.

Presentation of Freedom of the Borough to the York and Lancaster Regiment, May 1963. The regiment was officially disbanded in 1987. The mayor was Alderman Harry Dancer.

Staincross Freedom from Hunger Day, 1963. The two children collecting their drink are dressed as Bill and Ben the Flowerpot Men.

Another picture of the Staincross Freedom from Hunger Day, this time showing the disc jockey contest.

Pogmoor Feast prize giving, 1952.

Pogmoor Feast, 1952. Stan Bond is doing the high dive into the blazing tank.

Five
The North Wind Shall Blow

This snowball barricade was built in February 1963. Are the children barricading themselves in or out?

Locke Park in the winter of 1961-62, showing the old fountain in the Valley Gardens. Looking towards the main entrance, the Lodge can just be seen.

The spring of 1966, at Locke Park, with the back gates leading to Keresforth Hall Road in view.

Ionic columns in Locke Park, sometimes called the Corinthian columns, look down onto the Valley Gardens at the top of the ABC steps, 1962. The columns were acquired from the Commercial Building in Church Street.

Flash flooding on 14 June 1969 created havoc in Barnsley. On May Day Green, shoppers who were dressed for a hot humid day had to take what refuge they could.

Queen Street on the day of the 1969 flash flood, when over two inches of rain came down in ninety minutes. The fire brigade received over 150 calls for assistance.

Drivers risking their cars through the flooded Wellington Street. The Rose and Thistle public house could not open because the flood water ruined twelve barrels and twelve crates of beer.

The old Ebenezer chapel looking very picturesque with a light covering of snow. Sadly the chapel was closed on Easter Sunday, 30 March 1975.

A general view of Barnsley railway junction looking towards Manchester. This photograph was taken in early January 1952.

The Fleets, off Old Mill Lane, as it looked in 1962.

Taken in December 1962, the children of St Helen's Junior and Infants School, Monk Bretton, enjoy their playtime in the snow.

Samuel Matheson and his snowman. This photograph was taken in the playground of St Helen's Junior and Infants School in January 1963.

The children are warmly wrapped for their snowballing in March 1958.

Six

Where we Used to Work

Fenton's butchers, Barnsley Road, Cudworth. Ernie and his wife Irene are outside the shop, which is now Ian's butchers.

The BBCS. No, not the British Broadcasting Corporation but the Barnsley British Co-operative Society. This is the drug store which occupied No. 18 Cheapside from 1951 until 1960.

Co-operative drapery department at No. 21 Cheapside. This is a far cry from today's department stores. Can you remember your 'divi' number?

The corner shop is becoming a rare sight. The next four photographs show just a few of the corner shops that existed around Barnsley. This one was on Park Road. The photograph was taken in 1963.

This shop was on the junction of Wood Street and Harry Terrace, 1963.

A view here of the store at the corner of Wood Street and Heelis Street.

This store was on the corner of Heelis Street and Fleming Street in 1963, with Nos 103-111 Heelis Street to the left and Nos 19-25 Fleming Street to the right. All of these four establishments have now been demolished.

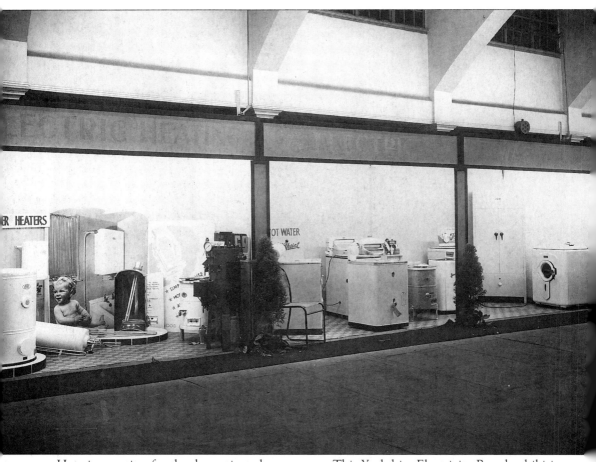

Here is a section for the domesticated among you. This Yorkshire Electricity Board exhibition was held in the Baths Hall, in the early 1950s. Note the very modern looking front loader washing machine.

These vacuum cleaners look like museum pieces compared with some of the space-age-looking machines we have today.

'The Master touch by the Mistress' is the caption given to these cookers.

From record players to farming equipment, the Yorkshire Electricity Board had something for everyone's needs.

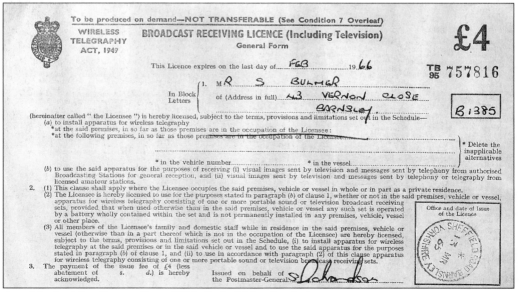

An old television license from 1966. Only £4 for the fee!

Staff at Worsbrough Coke Works, alias Barrow Coking Company, alias Barnsley Coking Company.

More staff at the Barnsley Coking Company. Do you know any of the faces in this photograph?

The next three photographs show what could have been a very sticky situation indeed. They feature the mud slide from Rockingham Tip to Shortwood in July 1967.

This shows how far the mud slide went and the date, 22 July 1967. This happened the year after Aberfan.

Keep going men, you are doing a grand job! The railway line covered by mud was the South Yorkshire Railway, later the LNER.

How many ladies can remember this sight? Here we have the hairdressing salon at the Co-op.

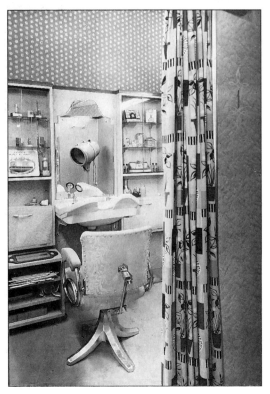

'Shampoo and set, madam? Please take a seat'.

Howbrook Garage, where Mr E. Wragg was proprietor.

More work in the garage, with Bob Gillam (on the right), who owned the garage in Platts Common.

Wilson and Longbottom, established in 1850, were makers of looms for the textile trade.

A view of a Wilson and Longbottom loom in action. In 1960 a joint company was formed with the Landsdowne Steel and Iron Company, of Pennsylvania, USA.

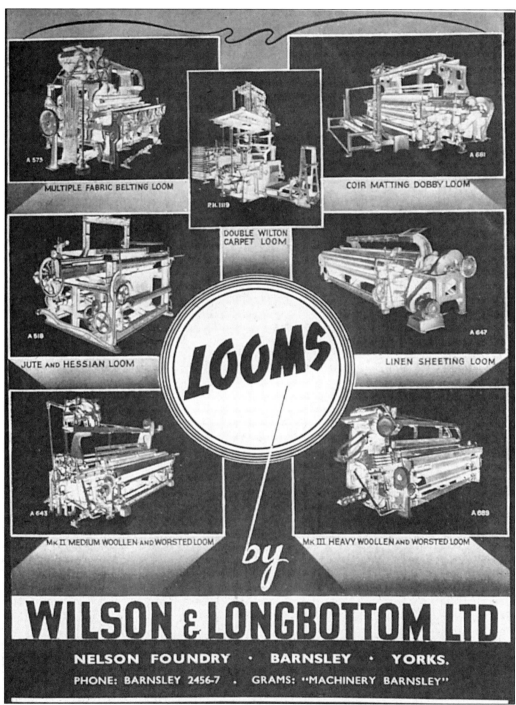

An advertisement in 1952 for Wilson and Longbottom's looms.

Rockingham Colliery in the 1960s. The sinking operations commenced in 1873 and the colliery was owned by Messrs Newton Chambers and Company. The pit was closed in 1980.

Barnsley Coking Plant, near Barrow Colliery, *c.* 1967. Production started at the plant in 1936 and it originally had fifty-one coke ovens. The plant ceased production in November 1975.

Here we have an action shot of a miner in a coal seam. This is a view of Wombwell Main Fenton Seam recorded on 22 February 1956. Notice the Ceag lamp on the miner's helmet.

Barnsley Main Colliery, looking towards the pit head from the Oaks Lane entrance, 1968.

A view of the Barnsley Canal, with Redfearns glassworks and the coal wharf in the winter of 1953/1954.

Cantors linen warehouse, Westgate. This photograph was taken in 1961, shortly before the warehouse was demolished.

Men at work. Here we can see the demolition of the Court House railway bridge, Eldon Street. This photograph was taken in 1961 by Mr Sid Jordan.

This evocative picture is of the air furnace at Wombwell Foundry, taken in April 1963.

The Dearne and Dove Canal, seen here south of Hoyle Mill. This photograph was taken as part of a survey made by the British Waterways Board in 1954. Notice how the level of the canal is well down.

The Dearne and Dove Canal again, this time showing a scene south of Stairfoot in 1954.

Clarkson's Brewery, as seen from Winn Street and Duke Street, November 1963. The Brewery was established in 1839 by Samuel Clarkson. The business was bought by Tennant Brothers in 1956 and finally owned by Whitbread after their takeover of Tennants in 1961. This photograph shows the scene just before the building was demolished.

An interior view of the brew house at Clarkson's Brewery in 1963.

Stairfoot Railway Junction, 31 May 1969.

The Screening Chamber on Pontefract Road, seen here in 1955.

A picturesque look at Reynolds and Wadsworth ironmongers on Market Hill, Barnsley.

Locke Park Hotel, seen here from the corner of Keresforth Hall Road in 1963. One can imagine that this must have been quite an establishment in its day!

Elsecar Main Colliery, seen here in the 1950s. The colliery was sunk in 1906 and closed in 1983.

A view of the Barnsley Brewery Company, which was founded in 1888, by seven Londoners after they acquired the Oakwell Brewery from Messrs Paul and Guy Senior. This photograph was taken in 1957.

An aerial view of the early life of the Carlton Industrial Estate. Plans for the estate were laid down in the late 1960s.

Seven

Scenic Barnsley

HE FOUNTAIN, LOCKE PARK, BARNSLEY. G.3182.

Many people in and around Barnsley sometimes think that it is a place with no landscape or scenery to please the eye. The photographs in this last chapter have been chosen to prove these people wrong. In this photograph can be seen an elegant view of the Locke Park Fountain in 1953.

Monk Bretton Priory, 1952. Founded in 1154 for the monks of the Order of Cluny, Monk Bretton Priory is not only a beautiful sight, but a great historical landmark in the Barnsley area.

Here, through the trees, can be seen more remains of the priory. During its residence, the priory would have housed a whole self-contained community. Part of the remains which we can see therefore, are those of the infirmary, kitchens and administrative buildings, as well as buildings of religious significance.

Through the archway. What sight could be more pleasing to the eye?

Even industrial sights have their significance and do not always mean a blot on the landscape. Mining in Barnsley was such an integral part of society that its role in our lives cannot be forgotten. Here we have a marvellous view looking from Dodds Corner across the Dearne Valley to Hoyle Mill, Barnsley Main Colliery and Oaks Viaduct in 1968.

Another view looking across the Dearne Valley, this time from Burton Bank, showing Redfearns' works on Harborough Hill Road in 1968.

Kexborough Village or Old Kexborough. Notice the advertisements on the shop front for Reckitt's Blue, Colman's starch, Colman's mustard and Fry's Pure Cocoa and chocolate.

This photograph shows the rear of the Red House and Redena House, taken in November 1960. They were to be found at the end of Bateman's Yard.

Oaks Viaduct in 1968, shortly before it was demolished. The Cudworth to Barnsley Push and Pull (Hull and Barnsley Line) ran across the viaduct. Barnsley Main Colliery can also be seen.

This photograph shows the five-arched aqueduct that Jessop decided in 1794, would carry the Barnsley Canal over the Dearne River. This view is part of what is now called the Dearne Valley Walk.

The Barnsley Canal's aqueduct in the process of being demolished. The abandonment warrant was granted in 1953.

This is the bridge over the canal on the Barnsley to Wakefield road in February 1964.

Redfearns can be seen in the background of this photograph of Old Mill Lane Bridge, taken in the winter of 1953/1954.

Barnsley Cemetery, showing one of the two churches that were listed buildings. Unfortunately, due to being in such a sad state of repair, both churches were demolished.

The walls and archway between the two churches at Barnsley Cemetery are all that remain to the present day.

An inspiring view of St Helen's Hospital, formerly the workhouse infirmary. This establishment was built in 1883 and closed its doors in 1977.

The Town Hall, taken from Church Street, in the late summer of 1967. Its reflection is shown in the plate glass window of what could be Watson's tobacconist. Shambles Street can be see in the background.

A view taken in 1961, looking out over Ward Green. In the distance can be seen Barrow Colliery and Chemical Plant.

Christmas 1963 and Barnsley Town Hall is looking quite splendid lit up against the dark night. The mayor's parlour lights are on and the Nativity scene is illuminated.